ASHRAM DHARMA

Swami Muktananda

A SIDDHA YOGA PUBLICATION
PUBLISHED BY THE SYDA FOUNDATION

Grateful appreciation goes to Peggy Bendet for preparing the text for publication; to Charity James, John Grimes, and Dayavrat Sharma for editorial assistance; to Cheryl Crawford for text and cover design; to Stéphane Dehais for typesetting, and to Sushila Traverse for overseeing production.

Copyright © 1975, 1995 SYDA Foundation.®
All rights reserved

(Swami) MUKTANANDA, (Swami) CHIDVILASANANDA, GURUMAYI, SIDDHA YOGA, and SIDDHA MEDITATION are registered trademarks of the SYDA Foundation.

Printed in the United States of America

First published in Hindi in 1968.
First published in English in 1975. Second edition 1995.

No part of this material may be reproduced or transmitted in any form or by any means, electronic or mechanical, including photocopy recording, or any information storage and retrieval system, without permission in writing from SYDA Foundation, Permissions Department, 371 Brickman Rd., South Fallsburg, New York 12779-0600, USA

ISBN 0-911307-38-9

Contents

Introduction by Swami Shantananda   v

Ashram Dharma   1

Gems of Ashram Dharma   33

Afterword   57

Glossary   61

Further Reading   65

Swami Muktananda

Introduction

Welcome to *Ashram Dharma!* In this book Swami Muktananda introduces us to the dharma, the principles of life, in an ashram and what is expected of us when staying in the ashram. "The whole purpose of an ashram," Swami Muktananda explains in these pages, "is to cleanse the mind of the impurities that creep into it from worldly pursuits, and to fill it with peace."

To derive the utmost benefit from the experience of being in an ashram — whether it's for an hour, a day, or several months — a sincere seeker tries to understand the traditions of the ashram and put into practice its essential discipline. Baba — as we called Swami Muktananda — has said, "In our ashrams all the activities are designed to help seekers intensify and improve their meditation. Recitation, chanting the divine Name, and even work, all help to focus the mind. If done in the spirit of selfless service to the ashram and the Guru, they serve to release divine love in the heart."

At the very core of the ashram is the state of the Guru. As Baba says in this book, the abodes of great saints are suffused by their own luminosity and love, a power that makes it possible for those who stay in such places to experience the Truth inside themselves. Shakti, as the scriptures call the divine Power, is the inner dynamo that brings about the transformation of seekers who stay in Siddha Yoga ashrams and bestows all the rewards for their efforts in spiritual practices. That was my experience of Gurudev Siddha Peeth, Baba's ashram at Ganeshpuri in India.

In 1972, when I first arrived at Gurudev Siddha Peeth, the ashram was relatively small, with fewer than a hundred people staying there. We always knew that no matter where we were in the ashram, Baba might appear at any time, striding up briskly, casting his sharp eye on whatever we were doing. He had an uncanny way of showing up just in time to correct something that could be done better. He would walk into the kitchen and from the doorway tell the cook to add a particular spice to what he was making, or look at a finance ledger and ask about the one item that was out of place. I recall once while I was working in the gardens Baba walked by and, for no apparent reason, told me, "Don't eat the green mangoes; they aren't good for your throat." Only the day before, the ashram manager had told me I *could* eat the green mangoes that had fallen from the trees. Later I found out the manager hadn't told Baba he had said that, and I certainly hadn't told Baba myself. Baba was showing his tremendous caring, but the primary effect of his all-encompassing attention was to inspire us to follow the discipline. The discipline, we learned, was crucial in training the mind to move away from the mundane, from its customarily limited goals, so that it could seek spiritual attainment.

The pivot of this discipline was the daily schedule, which to this day remains basically the same as it was when Baba first established it. Introspection, contemplation, service, study of the scriptures, and praising the Lord are pursuits that pervade the routine of a Siddha Yoga ashram, giving it the serene simplicity of a monastery. At the time I came to Gurudev Siddha Peeth, the rigor of the schedule was already well known in India and even abroad. A guide to the ashrams of India, compiled in the 1970s by a British publisher, described Gurudev Siddha Peeth as having "a very strict programme of meditation and chanting... which everyone is expected to follow." The schedule discouraged idlers from even thinking of visiting the ashram — and so it protected the ashram's sacred atmosphere.

For me as well as for many others who stayed there, it was precisely the discipline of following the ashram schedule that revealed the wonderful secrets of Siddha Yoga Meditation. My focus became so centered that it was relatively easy for me to fall into meditation, even while performing the physical chores of *seva*, or service to the ashram. I could feel the power of meditation overcoming my entire body and coloring with the magical presence of the sacred whatever I was doing. One day I wrote in my journal:

> *The manual work done under the open sun and the tightly packed schedule don't at all disturb the inner tranquility I am finding here. I can feel how effective the chants are. Without my understanding a word of what is being sung, the music takes over my whole attention, absorbing my mind until a meditative concentration comes over me easily, even in midst of the voices and the pounding*

> *drum. By the end of a chanting session, I am in a delicious kind of inner absorption that stays with me.*

"Everything I do is yoga," Baba once told us, "but you need a subtle eye to be able to understand." Baba used to teach this very well. With his entire being, he taught us how to be totally one-pointed while performing any kind of action, and how to perform it as an offering to God. Venkappa-ana, one of the oldest ashram residents, often described how in the ashram's early days, every morning by 2:30 Baba would be in the kitchen chopping vegetables, which he did with the speed and precision of a machine. After the chopping was over, Baba would take a bath and sit for meditation.

In later years Baba could be seen at that hour bowing to the lifesize statue of his Guru, Bhagawan Nityananda, in the ashram's temple; heading to the upper garden to feed the cows; or sitting in the darkness of the courtyard playing with the ashram puppies. By 3:00 A.M. most of the ashramites had gotten up and walked past the courtyard to the bathrooms and our cold water bucket baths. By 3:30 almost the whole ashram was meditating in the Cave, as we called a meditation room under

Baba's house, and also in Dhyana Mandir, the area that is now Baba's Samadhi Shrine. Baba used to walk through Dhyana Mandir with a flashlight to check how we were meditating. Often he would transmit his own divine energy into a seeker by brushing the person's forehead or touching them between the eyebrows. People could feel the Kundalini energy being awakened: they would have visions of inner light, or experience showers of love, or receive profound realizations. These early morning sessions of meditation would set the tone for the whole day. Those of us who lived in the ashram talked about our subtle experiences in the same way I remember once talking about news events or gossip. They were vital, they were real, they were the fabric of our lives — and, though these experiences of spirit weren't uncommon for us, they were always fresh.

Chanting, which began long before dawn, was usually done in the Bhagawan Nityananda Temple. At 4:15 A.M. an *āratī* was performed to Bhagawan and we chanted mantras Baba himself had compiled from the scriptures in his Guru's honor. Then the *Guru Gītā* chant began at 5:30. When Baba chanted with us, we had to keep perfect postures and remain completely still for the entire chant, which lasted an hour and a half. Only during the final *kīrtana, Shrī Krishna Govinda Hare Murare,* were we allowed to sway a bit. And if anyone nodded off while chanting, Baba would throw a small wooden block to wake him up.

The discipline had a great purpose: Baba was teaching us the power of *āsana* and *prānāyāma,* of controlling our posture and breath. With a still body and steady breath, one can tap into astonishing levels of inner bliss in chanting. Each morning as we sang the final *kīrtana,* we could look through the temple door or windows and watch the sun rising over the distant hills — a sublime moment in the day.

After 7:30 A.M. *seva* started. Baba gave *darshan* in the courtyard at mid-morning. Before lunch we chanted *Om Namah Shivāya* for twenty minutes and then another *āratī* was performed. Lunch was served at noon sharp in the Annapurna dining hall, in an atmosphere as sacred as that of the temple. Baba always insisted that food be revered as God. The ashram meals were prepared with a great deal of attention and love, and they were eaten in silence. Baba wouldn't permit anyone to waste as much as a grain of rice.

After lunch, everyone rested until

2:00 P.M. The recitation of the *Vishnu Sahāsranāma* took place at the end of the rest period, and at 2:45 was the afternoon *satsang* when letters from the devotees were read to Baba. The afternoon period of *seva* followed, until about 5:00.

A couple of times a week, Baba held question and answer sessions in the afternoon. These were the highlights of the week, when we had an opportunity to hear Baba's wisdom and practical advice on *sādhana*.

When the sun was about to set, there was an evening *āratī* in the temple. Supper followed, and afterward came the recitation of the *Shiva Mahimnā Stotram*. By 9:15 all the ashram lights were turned off for the night's rest.

Baba's model for conducting the ashram affairs and teachings was the *gurukula,* the home of the Guru, which in ancient times also served as a school. There have been ashrams where yogis gather to do their practices without the guidance of a master, and other ashrams where the master is not a supremely enlightened Siddha. However, in the great *gurukulas* of the Upanishads and Puranas, of the *Rāmāyaṇa* and *Mahābhārata,* a living Siddha Guru was the center of the students' activities. In Siddha Yoga ashrams, in the twentieth century, it is possible to have a firsthand taste of a genuine *gurukula* under an extraordinary Guru. This was true years ago with Swami Muktananda and it is true today with Swami Chidvilasananda, the lifelong disciple to whom Baba imparted his full yogic power before his death in 1982.

The message of *Ashram Dharma* is that the Guru's discipline, guided by divine grace, is the means to attain the joyous state of the Guru. This book contains the guidelines not only for staying in the ashram but also for leading a great life. In one of the question and answer sessions, Baba was asked about how someone who lives in the ashram should conduct himself once he leaves. Baba liked the question so much he had it repeated during the next session. He said, "An ashramite should not consider the ashram to be a particular place or area of land. To him the whole world is the ashram. Wherever you go, the ashram should go with you.... Wherever you go, you should listen to the inner voice that warns you against disregarding discipline. You should be following Truth, whether you are inside or outside the ashram. Let our lives become absolutely genuine. Let us get rid of all poses and pretensions. Wherever we are, we should follow a lifestyle that will fully protect us." Baba's legacy to us lies in principles that can bring harmony to our lives and restore to us the highest joy and fulfillment.

> *Swami Shantananda*
> *Shree Muktananda Ashram*
> *South Fallsburg, New York*
> *April 1995*

ASHRAM DHARMA

Meditation, one-pointedness of mind, and inner stillness are the essence of ashram dharma. Whether one is an ashramite devoted to service, a casual visitor, a devotee, a meditator, a lover of God, a seeker of divine knowledge, a scholar, or even a mere pretender pursuing sterile *siddhis* (supernatural powers), it is his duty to understand the traditions and discipline of the ashram through subtle reflection, and to practice that discipline earnestly. Those who do not follow those principles sin against the ashram dharma; they are dissolute and self-willed. Abodes of Siddhas, sacred places, and centers of pilgrimage are permeated by a divine power generated therein. It is the living, moving, talking power of God which, though established in its own glory, manifests itself by assuming a physical form for the sake of devotees. Those who live there permanently, stay for short periods, or even remember it with love, devotion, and reverence, are enveloped by this force.

It enters all seekers, devotees, and visitors and works within, bestowing the highest reward on them.

The character of any place is constantly remolded by the actions of its inhabitants. Through interaction, the place and its inhabitants become adapted to each other. If a saint lives there, it becomes filled with the influence of that saint. Wherever a great saint dwells, he endows that place with the character of his profound inner state. In fact, each abode of a Siddha bears the impress of his unique state. His Shakti envelops the place — sporting, manifesting itself, and generating ever-new bliss which never dies. His abode is not a mere brick-and-mortar structure, but an incarnation of himself in flesh and blood. There is no distinction between a holy place and its presiding saint. It is a Siddha who lends sanctity to a sacred place, sets up a standard of goodness by the example of his own actions, and gives authority to scriptures.

It is said that where Kakabhushundi, the great devotee of Lord Rama, lived even creatures without any devotional tendencies — birds, animals, *rākshasas,* hunters, and fishermen — became worshipers of the name of Rama. The entire atmosphere there was charged with the particles of the name of Rama. Every inch for miles around resounded with it. Its subtle power pervaded the trees, creepers, fruits, flowers and leaves, the soil and lakes, springs and streams. Partaking of the water, food, and fruits of such a sacred place, even smelling its flowers, awakens the spiritual energy in a human being.

Around Gautama Buddha, not only human beings, but even mutually hostile animals such as tigers and cows, peacocks and serpents, used to be quiet and nonviolent. There the divine force was manifested in its nonviolent and compassionate aspect, which throbbed, expanded, and broke into blossom in the atmosphere. Mahatma Gandhi was a great lover of truth and never uttered a false word. In his presence even the worst liars could not conceal themselves and used to confess honestly, "Mahatmaji, I am so-and-so. I have committed this crime."

In our own Ganeshpuri, my Gurudev, Bhagawan Shri Nityanandaji lived. He was a perfectly calm, supreme *avadhūt* with a loincloth and a towel as his only possessions; he remained solitary, continually immersed in the untainted state. He always sat serene, silent, and self-absorbed, radiating fearlessness and belonging to all. His manner has been described in the scriptures as follows: "He is said to be in the Shiva or *shambhavi* or *khecharī mudrā* whose mind has become motionless, transcending itself. As his mind no longer leans on any support, it is united with that which is beyond differences. His *prāna* has become calm and steady without any effort on his part to control or suppress it, but not for any attainment or *samādhi* experience. His eyes have become stable without practicing gazing at a fixed point — they no longer feel surprised at anything, nor are they attracted toward any object, however beautiful. Wherever they fall, they only see the light and loveliness of the Self. They are fixed not on any outer object but on their own essence. Such a one moves and sports freely in the sky of knowledge. He may be considered to be Shiva, Rama, Narayana, or Shakti. He perceives his own Self everywhere; to him the universe is full of Shiva, his devotees are full of Shiva, and all his acts reflect Shiva's glory. He lives in the highest transcendental state."

Such was the state of Bhagawan Nityananda. His eyes, though appearing to look outside, were directed inward. Being Self-realized, he experienced his own perfection and found complete fulfillment in his own Self. Being one with everything, he was always tranquil. The influence of his continual Self-recollection spread around him. Every sensitive person living near him appeared uncommonly peaceful and contented. The devotees coming from afar also bore a look of total fulfillment. One came thinking he would ask for a boon but went back without asking for anything — feeling that he had received everything. Another came bubbling with curiosity but returned satisfied without putting forward any questions. He who came to meditate obtained contentment without meditation. He who came to be enlightened experienced bliss without the aid of knowledge. A devotee felt love without performing any ritualistic worship and, while going away, remarked like one who had been charmed by a spell, "I had come for worship but I couldn't worship. I came to beg for help but I couldn't do that. Yet I feel as though I had performed worship and also received its fruit, as though I had obtained what I came to beg for. I have acquired faith and courage which I cannot explain."

This is the impact of the Ganeshpuri atmosphere — the magic of the power of spiritually charged particles or the subtle influence of the yogic fountain of bliss emanating from Shri Gurudev. Ganeshpuri rejoices and delights in the heart of Shri Nityananda contained in her folds.

The purer the visitors and residents of an ashram, the greater the manifestation of its power. Utterly lifeless is a holy region that is inhabited by those whose hearts are impure, who have no inclination for *sādhana*, no aptitude for the spiritual path, who do not desire inner peace and who only long for loaves and fishes — who, in short, are not worthy of living there. Nothing is reflected clearly in a dirty, dusty mirror, while in a clean mirror even the most minute reflection is clearly visible. Similarly, a heart endowed with purity, brightness, faith, and devotion fully unfolds and reflects the radiant force of a Siddha's abode or a place of pilgrimage. To live in a sacred center one has to have the requisite qualities and be worthy of it, as unworthy persons only eclipse its power. Just as one dominant tendency suppresses others, likewise those without yearning for liberation, averse to the ashram discipline, only caring for an easy life — those obtuse and stupid people who have no respect for the ashram routine and rules — push its divine luster underground. Though the

Chiti Shakti (divine Power) there is still in full bloom, its might and influence cannot be felt by all.

Those who live in an ashram are not all alike. Nor do the various visitors come with the same attitude. Some come, only eat and drink, and then leave. But an ashram is not a picnic resort; it follows a strict scriptural code. Once about eighty of us went on a pilgrimage to Rameshwaram. After staying there for a week and performing worship in accordance with traditional rites, we got ready to leave and asked the priest's customary permission. "You can certainly go, but you have to do a penance before leaving," he said.

"Penance! For what?" I asked. He replied, "Swamiji, Rameshwaram is a most sacred place. Each particle here has the merit of countless good actions accumulated in it. During a stay in such a holy center spitting, excretion of bodily waste matter, finding fault with others, talking ill of them, and harboring inauspicious fantasies, even through lack of vigilance, are all sinful deeds. Such lapses should not be committed within the limits of this sacred place, otherwise one loses the merit of all past noble deeds. If one is guilty of these wrong acts, though only inadvertently, one must ask for forgiveness and do penance to overcome their ill effects. This is what the *smriti shāstra* prescribes."

What that priest said is absolutely right. The scriptures say: "The sins committed at any other place are destroyed at a holy center, but those committed at a holy center stick tenaciously — it is difficult to wash them away."

Those residing at an ashram should possess the spirit of service and see only innocence in others' failings. Those who are themselves impure detect impurities readily because they have an affinity with them. But he who leads a pure and austere life at an ashram soon gets rid of his shortcomings, becoming taintless. Just as the wicked readily look for vices, likewise the virtuous are immediately attracted toward virtues. Therefore everyone living at an ashram should be pure and innocent.

Our ashram has a number of bright, purifying, ennobling features which promote strength and radiance, yet surprisingly the faultfinders, instead of being drawn toward them, only pick those features they can criticize. Even during a short stay they detect faults in the residents who are sincere and rendering excellent service. If they themselves were noble and pure-hearted, why would they pick holes in others? On the contrary they would see their goodness, taintlessness, and sincerity.

Our ashram library has excellent books in different languages. The criticizing types show no interest in the deep knowledge contained in them. They do not respond to the beauty of the orchards and trees, the fertility of the branches bending to the ground with their rich fruits, the loveliness and fragrance of abundant flowers, and the holiness of the cows. Nor are they fascinated by the white peacocks or their dancing, or by the bright, pure, and pretty fish, which are so lively, friendly, and bold that they love to eat from human hands. They ignore the ashram dogs, who are intelligent and pure and understand the human heart. The lovely creepers emerging from under the stones, the beautiful and rare trees, such as the white coral, white swallow wort, white beech, white oleander, and chitrika, which the ashramites have reared with hard toil and extraordinary fortitude, do not speak to their hearts. The eleven varieties of champa, twelve varieties of chameli, twenty-two kinds of jasmine, forty kinds of roses, twenty kinds of Nilgiri eucalyptus, Japanese bamboos, Zanzibar plantains, eighteen varieties of coconuts, one hundred and eight varieties of mangoes — all these lovely, luscious, and delicious things only invite their criticism. They react adversely to everything. It reminds me of a saying: Good people look only for virtue, the wicked ones for vice. The noble ones always notice only the truth and goodness of others. Those who can only see faults are vicious and evil under the surface although they may appear to be good and virtuous. In this context, I am reminded of a story. Once a great architect built a palace for a king. The palace was a beautiful work of art with all its fine carvings, sculptures, and paintings. Kings admired it for its richness and splendor; ministers, for its uncommon library. Architects appreciated its architectural beauty; generals, its armory; and artists, its art. But once a sweeper came there, he looked only at a lavatory and exclaimed, "Disgusting! How dirty!" The moral of this story is that one notices only what one is interested in.

    I am also reminded of a dialogue from the *Mahābhārata*. Lord Vasudeva (Krishna) asks Yudhishthira and Duryodhana a question in turn. He says to Yudhishthira, "O righteous one, how many sinners are there in this gathering?" Yudhishthira replies,

"Lord, this is an assembly of fortunate and pious people. How can there be a sinner here?" Then Lord Krishna asks Duryodhana, "O King, how many virtuous souls are there in this gathering?" Duryodhana replies, "Vasudeva, everyone here is vicious and without light. I can see only sinners all around me in this court." These are two attitudes: one looking toward heaven and the other toward hell; one seeing goodness and purity in all, and the other seeing vice even in the innocent. It gives great happiness to be irreproachable in one's conduct and to see innocence even in vice. The viewpoint one adopts shows one's quality and worth.

The impressions of a man's actions of previous lives remain embedded in his heart. The human psyche is clogged with perverse impressions of countless births, as a result of which one finds a reflection of one's own feelings in others. It is one's own mind that sees vice in innocence, impurity in purity, and destruction in joy. Just as the reflection of gathering clouds is dark even in the clear water of a lake, so is the case with such a mind. Therefore one should behave calmly, with love and affection, without a faultfinding attitude. As soon as one enters a Siddha's ashram, one's worldly propensities should fall away, and the mind should become pure and ready to grasp spiritual truths. Just as we open all the doors and windows of a room to let in light and air, similarly the mind should be thrown open completely to the divine Shakti. One should perceive the Chiti expanding and sporting in all the ashram trees and nourishing their roots.

The tendencies in the mind predispose the mind to look for similar characteristics in others. Good people take a long time to find whatever failings there may be in the visitors and residents of the ashram; the bad ones not only see the faults straightaway, but to them even some good qualities appear objectionable. Utterly futile is the visit to an ashram of one who, lacking a good attitude, goes away with his mind even more impure than before, obsessed with the darker side of everything, and complaining loudly, "Oh, there are terribly filthy spots in that ashram. As I went in, everyone was sitting silently. No one had the courtesy to welcome me or even talk to me." Such a person would leave an ashram as empty-handed as he was when he arrived. He is not only unable to show his good qualities but he cannot escape the tyranny of his defects even for a short while. Nor does he have the openness to see even briefly the merits of an ashram. He goes to a holy place, eats and drinks, wastes time and money, and leaves without any benefit. Remember that the habit of faultfinding brings about one's decline.

From a center of pilgrimage, a Guru, a deity, and an ashram, a seeker receives what he offers. The atmosphere of a Siddha's abode is charged with enormous force. It has its impact on a person as soon as he enters it and begins to recast him in its own mold. One whose heart is completely pure will fully respond to the characteristic feeling dominating a holy place.

All the *siddhis* and *riddhis* (supernatural powers and worldly attainments) used to dance attendance on Shri Gurudev Bhagawan Nityananda. Large quantities of bananas, seasonal fruits and flowers, sweets, toffees and biscuits of different varieties, and other articles were offered to him. People made these offerings out of their affection and reverence for him, and according to their custom, tradition, taste, and means. As a result, clothes, fruits, and various other things used to lie openly for a long time near the door. They were distributed at the right time in accordance with a certain system. Some spectators would raise a question, asking, "Why are so many things lying here? Baba doesn't distribute them among visitors? What use does a saint have with such a rich hoard?" The truth is that while the devotees bring offerings of their own accord, lovingly and joyfully, and feel gratified, the onlookers smolder in the inner fire of spiritual privation, having only doubts, jealousy, malice, greed, and envy to give.

In an ashram, an offering coming from a devotee living in any part of the world must not be rejected; on the contrary, it should be considered to be a part of God's treasure of righteous wealth and be distributed in a spirit of service, according to scriptural injunctions, bearing in mind the worth of the one who receives it. Even a single penny coming as a gift should be regarded as belonging to dharma and God. He who gives from a pure motive offers his wealth to God. In fact, the scriptures hold that whatever is offered to God is God, belongs to God, and its giver is also God. According to the scriptures: "Shiva is the giver, Shiva is the enjoyer. Shiva is, indeed, this entire universe. Shiva is the sacrificer, and the sacrifice. And that Shiva am I." He who gives, he who receives, and the offering itself are all divine. A religious temple or holy place and all its belongings are only different forms of religion itself—this is the right attitude.

The ashram belongs to all — be they pious, scholarly, learned, poetic, or spiritually inclined; foolish, low, sinful, or vicious. All come with the hope of overcoming the negative consequences of their past bad deeds and deriving positive benefit. Everyone, whether a cheat, priest, or thief, wants to be relieved of his troubles and find peace. Whoever may come, the ashram remains what it is. It does not alter its character and faith for anyone. The ashram is independent of both good and bad — a place of inner freedom. It is like the Ganges in which a pure and virtuous person has a perfectly peaceful dip, and where a despicable, wicked one also washes away the dirt of his sins. But the Ganges treats both equally. It is her nature, her function, to impart purity and coolness to all who come. Can she be held responsible if someone is drowned owing to his own stupidity or past misdeeds? Similarly, the ashram doors are open to all, but everyone must observe its rules and discipline. In this quiet place one should sit silently and have a pure mind.

Ashram residents generally remain absorbed in the performance of their duties.

They have neither the time nor the habit to look for faults. In the ashram everyone is taught to remain aware of the omnipresence of Shiva—to look upon everyone as Shiva, not to consider anyone different from Shiva. One should see Shiva in the body and mind, in wealth, and in everything, inside and out. Almost everyone at the ashram follows this principle. Those who are engrossed in their various tasks, who keep their minds fixed on the inner goal, can have no time to detect sinful and impure tendencies. Only idle fools have the leisure for this.

Our ashram is not the monopoly of one particular caste, class, or nationality. It is meant for all — women as well as men, the old as well as the young; but everyone must live here with restraint and purity, obeying the ashram discipline. Here one's qualities alone are worshiped, not one's gender or age. For this reason all those who are disciplined, having good character and a sincere longing for enlightenment, can live here. God has created everyone alike. Man, driven by his own evil predilections, creates differences and inequalities and weeps and wails, falling prey to misery.

It is essential for the ashramites to honor each visitor as a form of the Lord. One cannot acquire all virtues as soon as one enters the ashram. People come here to cultivate self-restraint and discipline, moral principles, and purity of character and conduct. It is everyone's duty to keep his heart open to virtues. Concealing one's own faults but disclosing those of others is hardly desirable. The more one conceals one's failings, the deeper they take root and the more rapidly they grow — like crocodiles and other deadly aquatic creatures — in the clear pool of the heart. Weaknesses become worse if concealed, but they are easily overcome if admitted without protest. In the same manner, the more we hide our good qualities like a precious treasure, the more they grow like a science that is learned secretly. I do not, however, suggest that virtues not be expressed in action, but these should not be unnecessarily talked about for self-glorification. One must praise others' good qualities; this nourishes one's own, like food. Therefore, after coming to the ashram, one's constant endeavor should be to get rid of one's failings and imbibe good qualities.

An ashram manifests the divine glory. Here the radiant, blazing Chiti Shakti carries on Her sublime work. The ashram may appear to be an ordinary place to our physical eyes, but its every leaf, flower, fruit, tree, and creeper is pervaded by Kundalini Shakti. Therefore, one should live here with vigilance in thought, speech, and action. The different objects in the ashram which may appear to be mere matter are not so. They appear so owing to the spectator's own insensitivity. They have been immersed in the lake of Consciousness for a long time. Therefore, those who live here with self-control, faith, and purity will also be immersed in that lake of Consciousness.

In an ashram most of the time should be spent in meditation and contemplation of God. One should not fritter away one's precious time in a precious place on eating and drinking, sleeping, gossiping, and talking idly. How miserable is man's lot! At home and in the streets, he lives with a distracted mind, uttering abusive terms and unbecoming words, sleeping lazily and wasting his time. And if he is fortunate enough to visit a sacred place, he behaves in exactly the same manner in which he behaves at home, in his office or factory. What a great pity! The whole purpose of an ashram is to cleanse the mind of the impurities that creep into it from worldly pursuits, and to fill it with peace.

When entering an ashram, one should

be fully aware of one's true value. Enter it in a civilized, disciplined, calm, and humble manner. Let the mind be free from worldly burdens. Otherwise, it will be no different from going to a railway station, club, theater, or coffee shop where one makes a lot of noise and comes back feeling empty, desiccated, and miserable. The more one follows the discipline of a sacred place, the higher will one rise, the more intense will be one's longing for God.

The residents of an ashram, whether renunciants or householder-aspirants, should always be vigilant and ensure that their *sādhana* is not impeded. They should carry on their routine without interruption, feel grateful to the ashram, eat, relax, and behave in a balanced manner. They must not fritter away their calm and silence by indulging in futile arguments and idle chatter. If you earn only fifty *paise* daily but spend ten *rupees,* what can you save?

There are many who continue to commit wicked actions for years. They think of God for a short while, then they look toward the sky wondering why they are still without the promised fruit, why a chariot is not descending from heaven to take them. I am reminded of a humorous poem I read long ago, which says: If you remove one straw from a back-breaking burden on a camel or an elephant, will it make a difference? If you throw one clove out of a sinking boat, will that lighten its weight significantly? If you deal in *lakhs* of *rupees,* what does a quarter of a *rupee* mean?

These are childish fancies. Move about in the ashram freely, but always keep your mind pure. Don't let it become blemished, or be overcome by jealousy, sloth, sensuality, and garrulousness. Remain alert at every moment. The moment it is diverted, bring it back toward the objective with a resolute effort. Lord Krishna says in the *Bhagavad Gītā:* "Whenever the restless and unsteady mind begins to wander, restrain it and bring it under the control of the Self." Concentration and purity of mind can be achieved through practice and dispassion. Remember that a spark can spread into a wild fire, burning an entire forest away; one drop of curd can turn a large quantity of milk sour; similarly, unholy thoughts not curbed become in time deep-seated and completely distract the mind from meditation. A distracted mind makes a person insipid and sick at heart, squeezing all joy out of his life.

Company has great power. One aphorism in the *Bhakti Sūtras* of Narada, the divine seer, says that passions like lust and wrath may appear as tiny ripples at first, but through bad company, they swell into a vast ocean. There is a similar verse in the *Rāmacharita-mānasa,* depicting the glory of association with good people: "The happiness of heaven and of liberation put together is nothing compared to the happiness that one gets from a little *satsang.*" For this reason, Narada says, "I urge you to seek the company of great saints, to seek their company alone."

Often someone tells me: "Babaji, one day I had very deep meditation. I experienced such blissful contentment as I had never felt before in my life. But of late, for quite some time I haven't been able to get the same meditation again. I do not know what has happened." My reply is, "Brother, the first day the divine qualities, such as noble feeling, fervent devotion, unwavering faith, and intense reverence, had made your heart tender, loving, sweet, and pure. Besides, you were quite keen on experiencing a spiritual state. For these reasons, your mind did not offer any resistance and simply became absorbed in meditation. After that you should have further cultivated respect for the ashram, devotion to God, faith in your Guru, and surrender to him, but you did not. On the contrary, you made your mind impure once again by looking for faults in the ashramites and criticizing the visitors. When your mind became occupied with these, where was the scope for devotion or meditation? You began to degenerate steadily until you reached your present level of inner emptiness." A true aspirant must not behave like this. Knowing how the mind works, he must always remain alert and vigilant.

Once I heard from a great man during his lecture that the milk of a lioness can be kept only in a gold vessel. In containers of other metals, it makes holes and runs out. Similarly, a seeker whose mind is one-pointed, free from wanderings among objects, whose heart has drunk the nectar of love for his Guru, is a gold vessel, fit to be an abode of devotion to God and the divine Power and grace received through *shaktipāt*. A mind free from thoughts is in meditation. A mind free from external occupations and steady in all circumstances is a mind in meditation. Love blooms in its fullness in a mind that is inward-turned and free from change and attachments. Juice oozes out of the *chandrakant* gem when it is exposed to the moon; the *suryakant* gem melts when exposed to the sun; likewise a mind completely turned toward God melts and dissolves at the divine touch. My advice is: Brother, don't spend your life in vain. Your transient body is of hardly any use once it deteriorates. Do not allow it to become lazy. Whether you are wealthy or poor, do not give way to lethargy, apathy, sloth, and inertia. Work hard and be self-reliant.

There is no one to command me now but even so I lead a most orderly life. No one has to wake me up in the morning. I get up without fail at 3:00 every day. I clean my lavatory myself. I attend to every duty on time. I am punctually present at the recitations of the *Guru Gītā*. I always take a frugal meal at a fixed time. I never keep late hours. Even if there is nothing to do I do not retire to sleep or eat irregularly. I attend to the ashram work to the best of my ability and I am quite dependable. I do not let any of the things offered so lovingly by devotees be neglected, spoiled, or ruined. The smallest article is given as much importance as the most precious one. I try to ensure that everyone in the ashram sleeps, gets up, and eats punctually, remains silent and alone even in the midst of a crowd, sits calmly and steadily, talks softly and a little, only when it is necessary, continues to repeat his mantra without a break as much as possible, and lives a pure and austere life.

Nowadays even in ashrams, inner freedom and work for salvation are giving way to licentious and unrestrained behavior. In an ashram it is not right to indulge in sensual pleasures in the name of love or to be a shameless slave of carnal cravings. An ashram is not a place for sexual indulgence or dispute and argument; nor is it a stage for a couple to enact the drama of their married life. Wretched is he who cannot observe discipline and restraint even in an ashram. That so-called love that is immodest, unrestrained, self-willed, and trapped in the mire of lust is unworthy and despicable, only fit to be spat at. If we cannot live austerely even in holy places and ashrams, but remain entangled in our worldly concerns during our short stay there, are we human?

Do not become an obstacle to others' growth. We should conduct ourselves in such a modest and undisturbing manner that others are not distracted. We should live quietly and exercise control over speech and actions so that neither does the ashram become corrupted nor do we become degraded. About three years ago I visited a very big ashram. I liked most of its features, including the college. I was, however, enraged at the immodest way of dressing. Girls at an ashram should not be dressed like frivolous club dancers. An ashram has a special decorum and culture. How one talks, sits, stands, eats, drinks, and dresses here has its own impact. If the body is not properly covered, it appears to be indecent and repulsive in spite of its beauty.

Moreover, it enhances the body-consciousness in oneself and others. For this reason I repeat again and again that the inner being and the outer form of an ashramite should conform to the ashram standards.

That person is really great who has renounced pride, jealousy, and ignorance; who acquires as much humility as wealth and status. A cloud bends low when saturated with water, a tree bends low when laden with fruit. Why should man, then, be proud of his possessions? Gandhiji, who is worthy of all our reverence, used to clean his lavatory, sweep, and do other menial jobs himself. One need not be ashamed of doing one's own daily work. During your stay in the ashram, you should clean your room, lavatory, and bathroom, and make your bed yourself. Everything here should be regarded as God's and used with love and care. This applies to every article in your room — cushions, sheets, covers, mats, tripods, water flasks, and glasses. Keep them clean and in order. Never depend on others for your work. Do not lose what you have gained from meditation, prayer, chanting, and study of sacred books, by demanding service from others. Selfishness, seeking comfort for oneself while depriving others of it, and making others clean your toilet and utensils — these are contrary to ashram dharma and should be eschewed.

    Reflect on the significance of an ashram. It is the extended body of a Siddha, yogi, saint, seer, or sage. Go there with a desire to serve and consider every opportunity of service a gift of God's grace. An ashram is not a place for rest and sensual indulgence. It is not the house of your parents-in-law where you are indulged and fussed over. It is neither a theater for your amusement and recreation nor a club for idle talk and gossip.

    While at home, you spend your time filling your stomach, gratifying your senses, occupying your mind in all sorts of pursuits, worries and anxieties, wild hopes, anger and irritation, cunning, intrigue, and sensual indulgence. You continually conduct yourself in the same manner when you leave your home — in your office or factory, or in the company of friends. You thus harm yourself as well as others. At least, do not carry this mentality to an ashram or a place of pilgrimage. Otherwise, years pass and you remain deluded, stupid, and careless, doing at an ashram what you do at home. Brother, do not waste your time, as time is infinitely precious.

I shall say one thing more. Wherever you go, you will see your past, present, and future attitudes reflected there. One established in God sees His play all around; a devotee of Krishna sees Him dancing joyfully everywhere. A divine lover perceives blissful, divine forms surrounding him; one devoted to the Guru perceives his everlasting delight in every place. For a vicious fellow the world is full of vice; for a cheat it is full of fraud; for a depraved one it is full of sin. To a scientist it is nothing but atomic energy. But scientific truth is not the final Truth. In reality, the world is an expansion of the perfect Being, a splendid display of supreme joy; it communicates the divine knowledge that all creatures are the same, each being equally divine. It is a great means of the realization of joy beyond the senses, a school where one can learn how to have a perfect experience of the Perfect.

Ordinary people treat it as a mere world, seeing it as full of differences. But it is a sphere saturated with the power of yoga, a manifestation of the Divine Soul; nay, a boundless ocean vibrating its countless forms.

Man is only a ray emanating from Chiti, the source of light; he should become one with that source and attain full Consciousness and bliss. O men, transform yourselves. Do not project your own defects onto others. A devotee of Rama fills his heart with Rama, makes His image, waves lights to Him, meditates resolutely on Rama, and talks about Him. Similarly, a faultfinder imputes failings to others, remains obsessed with faults whether he be at home or at an ashram, and disparages others in a firm tone. A person corrupts his own heart by wrong attitudes, turning it into an ocean of vices. How will he ever experience heaven when he always speaks evil, sees evil, and contemplates evil? To a blind man bright day is dark night, to a deaf person melodious music is dead silence, to a stomach patient the most delicious food is tasteless; likewise, to a faultfinder heaven is hell, the world of Vishnu is the world of death, and a sacred place is a den of impurities.

O seekers, your own mind is your heaven as well as hell. Sometimes I apply a little *hīna* scent offered with love by a devotee. Wherever I go its fragrance goes with me. The purity of one's heart is its true fragrance. It accompanies one everywhere. If your mind becomes taintless, it will be illumined with light. Fill your heart for a while with love, affection, and purity while you are in this very body, in this very place, here and now. Then you will experience for yourself the presence of Rama within and without, everywhere. You will be continually immersed in meditation, undergoing yogic processes and feeling bliss. This is your true paradise of Vaikuntha, the meaning of *Namah Shivāya*, the essence of knowledge, and the sweetness of love.
This is the gift you receive from Shiva, Hari, or the Guru; the goal of aspirants, devotees, and disciples. This is pure ethics, the teaching of all religions, and the message of the Upanishads. This is the miracle of the Guru's grace, the meaning of salvation or Self realization. Therefore see the universe in yourself and yourself in the universe and annihilate your ego, your separate identity. Let your Self become the cosmos and the cosmos become your Self: become the Universal Soul.

Gems of
Ashram Dharma

1. *Continue to reflect and contemplate by yourself in seclusion.*

2. *Do not turn the ashram into a land of pleasure and license. Conduct yourself according to the sanctity of the place.*

3. *Observe the ashram discipline, remaining still and calm before you are told to do so. Teach the same to your friends, children, and spouse.*

4. *Observe silence. When necessary, speak the minimum in a low tone. Silence is a great achievement.*

5. *Time is most precious. Do everything punctually.*

6. *Take food in measured doses, as you take medicine.*

7. | *G*ive up pride and egoism. Humility leads to perfection, while conceit is self-deception.

8. | *T*he body is mere flesh which has no value when separated from the spirit. Engage it in ceaseless service.

9. | *K*eep on donating your labor; charity is the ladder to heaven.

10. *Do not concern yourself with faults. Do not look for shortcomings in visitors. To find fault with others is to degrade oneself.*

11. *Do not praise yourself in the presence of others. Be praiseworthy.*

12. *Do not live so shamelessly that others may look down upon or detest you.*

13. *Keep your mind untainted, free from thoughts. The divine qualities of this place will overpower you.*

14. *Meet whomever you wish, but acquire only his divine virtues.*

15. *Participate joyfully in the ashram routine and activities — the prayers, recitations, and chants of divine Names. If you have no taste for these, move immediately to a guest house.*

16. *Inside the ashram do not disturb the calm of others by the heavy stamping of your shoes, clatter of your wooden sandals, and rustle of your clothes. Walk quietly and speak slowly and softly.*

17. *You will receive as much respect as you show to others. By honoring others, you are not doing a favor to others but to yourself.*

18. *Status acquired through degrees or office is transient. The same Self dwells in all.*

19. *First practice yourself what you want to teach others.*

20. *You may be somebody's boss in your office or factory but not in the ashram or the world outside.*

21. *Love others if you wish to be loved by them.*

22. *First reform yourself completely, then others. He who has discrimination, but nothing material to give to others, can induce others to give liberally.*

23. *First teach your own family to be good and wise, and then teach others.*

24. *Instead of filling your house with things begged humbly from others, eliminate want by renunciation and self-control.*

25. *Study of scriptures, purity of heart and conduct, and simple and unaffected living lead to inner peace.*

26. *Find respect, peace, and love within yourself. Do not seek these from others.*

27. *Whether you are a king or a beggar, you will have to leave all your possessions behind. Think about what will go with you after your death.*

28. *Always work industriously, otherwise you will fall prey to sloth. Do not become dull and lazy on receiving God's grace.*

29. *If divine virtues always keep company with you, they will bring you peace and happiness. They can neither be taxed nor snatched away by any political party.*

30. *He alone can command who obeys.*

31. *Follow the ashram rules faithfully. These are indeed steps to the city of salvation.*

32. *Do not hate anyone who comes to the ashram.*

33. *Welcome every visitor to the ashram. Who knows in what form the Lord may appear?*

34. *Heaven is certainly not the fruit of sin, nor meditation or fame the fruit of idleness.*

35. *Do not make your bad actions look like good ones and in that way misguide others.*

36. *Cultivate the attitude of seeing the Divine in each other.*

37. *Regard the world as an image of God, and a holy place as an image of a saint.*

38. *Keep your place in the ashram tidy and in order. Regard everything you use as God's.*

39. *Each particle and atom in the ashram is permeated by the supreme Chiti Kundalini, the supreme Maya Shakti or Yogini. Honor Her at every moment and that will remove all obstacles in the way of your meditation.*

40. *S*tudy the Absolute Science inscribed
in the vines and creepers.

41. *S*it in your seat peacefully
and in a relaxed way,
without touching anyone else.

42. *Y*our body does not gain strength simply
because somebody else is healthy;
in the same manner, no purpose
of yours can be served by
another's miraculous powers.

43. *Continue to cleanse yourself by* tapasya *with full eagerness.*

44. *Do not neglect the sound of the great mantra even for a moment.*

45. *Repeat an external mantra until the mantra arises from within.*

46. *Become so pure,
pursue your* sādhana
*with such intensity,
be so absorbed in meditation
that all seven constituents
of your body may resound
with the mantra.*

47. *Fill your mind with the knowledge
of Truth and let your senses function
with discrimination.
If the divine Shakti becomes
fully active within you,
it will be easily transmitted
to others. You need not struggle
to spread its influence.*

48. *Just as bubbles and waves
arise in the same water,
likewise all diversities
appear in the same Being.
The supreme Truth is only one.*

49. *Birth and death are twin children
of the same mother.
Do not be bothered by them.
They will continue coming and going.*

50. *There is no objective world without "I." If "I" goes, that also vanishes. That which remains is the blissful Self. Therefore renounce not your home, but "I" and "him." Your home is a most valuable school.*

51. *The external world is known with the eyes, the eyes are known with the mind, the mind with the reason, and the Knower of the reason is the Father of the universe. And you are that Shri Guru Nityananda.*

52. *The one who is the unmoving witness of the activities of the waking state, the dream state and deep sleep is not made of flesh, nor is it anyone's monopoly. That witness is called the Self; That art Thou. Why in your ignorance do you lament, "I will die, oh, I will die."*

53. *The ashram values its discipline. If you love it, the ashram will also love and respect you.*

54. *Enjoy eternal bliss which is far, far away from sensual pleasures.*

55. *Just as one does not need much paraphernalia for sleep, similarly it is not necessary to have many mental processes for meditation.*

56. *Meditate during quiet hours. Whatever you envision in meditation, consider it to be your deity.*

57. *Respect the ashram as the extended body of Shri Gurudev.*

58. *None is more worthy of remembrance than God and Guru. Contemplate them every moment.*

59. *There is no deity superior to the Guru, no gain better than the Guru's grace, no* japa *more rewarding than remembering the Guru, no state higher than meditation on the Guru — therefore become a true child of the Guru.*

60. *Bliss is true devotion, bliss is one's own true form — to be aware of this is to revel in the inner Self. The permanent state of immersion in the Self is divine joy, it is the essence of Muktananda.*

Afterword

On the occasion of Swami Muktananda's sixtieth birthday, in May 1968, he distributed as a gift to all who attended his birthday celebration the inspiring essay and aphorisms on discipline that comprise the text of *Ashram Dharma*. The original publication contained sixty aphorisms, one for each year of Baba's life, and the verse on the following pages, listed as number sixty-one, in honor of the year ahead.

61. *Now I count sixty-one:*
counting minute by minute,
an hour is gone;
counting hour by hour,
a day is gone;
counting the days,
Monday, Tuesday... a week is gone;
counting the weeks, a month;
and a whole year has passed.
Counting this way,
all of childhood is gone.
And without noticing it,
youth is also gone.
How intoxicated I was in my youth,
but now, full sixty years are over.
I ate a lot and satisfied my thirst—
who knows where it all went.
What I ate did not stay with me.
What I saw did not last.

*Splendor, beauty, strength, and
majesty — everything is gone.
What is left is very little and of no use.
Waking up now, I turn my face.
Showing my back to the world,
turning toward myself,
entering the inner door,
I start for home,
where there is no weeping,
no suffering, no agitation;
there is only the one endless,
full, divine, pure, calm, and still ocean,
filled with Muktananda,
the bliss of freedom of* Om So'Ham.

*Your own inner flame,
Your own dear Baba*

Guide to Sanskrit Pronunciation

Vowels

Sanskrit vowels are categorized as either long or short. In English transliteration, the long vowels are marked with a bar above the letter and are pronounced twice as long as a short vowel. The vowels *e* and *o* are also pronounced like long vowels.

Short:	Long:
a as in cup	*ā* as in calm
i as in give	*ī* as in seen
u as in full	*ū* as in school

Consonants

The main variations from the way consonants are pronounced in English are the aspirated consonants. These are pronounced with a definite *h* sound. The *dh*, for example, is pronounced as in roadhouse; the *bh* as in abhor. For a detailed pronunciation guide, see *The Nectar of Chanting*, published by SYDA Foundation.

Glossary

avadhūt: A saint who has transcended body-consciousness and whose behavior is not bound by ordinary social conventions.

Bhagawan: (*lit.* the Lord) One endowed with the six attributes of infinity: spiritual power, righteousness, glory, splendor, knowledge, and renunciation. A term of great honor. Swami Muktananda's Guru is known as Bhagawan Nityananda.

Ganges: The most sacred river of India. The Ganges is said to purify all sins of anyone who bathes in its holy waters.

Hari: A name of Lord Vishnu, one of the Hindu trinity of gods, representing the supreme Reality as the sustainer of the universe.
See also Krishna, Rama.

japa: (*lit.* prayer uttered in a low voice) Repetition of a mantra, either silently or aloud.

khecharī mudrā: An advanced yogic pose in which the tongue is thrust back and up. This *mudrā* pierces one of the *granthis* (subtle inner knots), causing the meditator to experience *samādhi* and taste divine nectar.

kīrtana: A song that praises or glorifies the divine Name.

Krishna: (*lit.* the dark one; the one who attracts irresistibly) The eighth incarnation of Lord Vishnu, whose teachings are contained in the *Bhagavad Gītā*.

Kundalini: (*lit.* the coiled one) The supreme Power, primordial Shakti, or energy, that lies coiled at the base of the spine in the subtle system of each human being. Once awakened Kundalini initiates various yogic processes that bring about the purification and rejuvenation of the entire being.

lakh: A Hindi term meaning a hundred thousand.

Maya Shakti: The power of illusion; the indefinable power of the supreme Being that projects the illusion of the universe.

Namah Shivāya: (*lit.* I bow to Shiva) The Sanskrit mantra of the Siddhas, *Om Namah Shivāya,* is known in the scriptures as the great redeeming mantra because of its power to grant both worldly fulfillment and spiritual realization. *Om* is the primordial sound; Shiva denotes the Lord who dwells in every heart.

paise: The smallest Indian coin. One hundred *paise* make a *rupee*.

prāna: The vital life-sustaining force of both the body and the universe.

Puranas: The eighteen sacred texts containing legends and hymns concerning the creation of the universe, the incarnations of God, the instructions of various deities, as well as the spiritual legacies of ancient sages and kings.

rākshasas: Demonic beings.

Rama: The seventh incarnation of Lord Vishnu, Rama is seen as the embodiment of righteousness and is the object of great devotion. The story of his life is told in the epic *Rāmāyana.*

rupee: The standard unit of Indian currency.

sādhana: A spiritual discipline or path; practices, both physical and mental, on the spiritual path.

samādhi: The meditative state of absorption in the Absolute.

satsang: (*lit.* in the company of the Truth) The company of saints and devotees; a gathering of devotees for the purpose of chanting, meditating, and listening to scriptural teachings.

seva: (*lit.* service) Selfless service; work offered to God.

Shakti: Force, energy; spiritual power; the dynamic aspect of God.

shaktipāt: (*lit.* the descent of grace) The transmission of spiritual power, or Shakti, from the Guru to the disciple; spiritual awakening by grace.

shambhavi mudrā: A state of spontaneous *samādhi* in which the vision, though the eyes are open, is focused within. It is the usual state of a Siddha, also known as the Shiva *mudra*.

Shiva: A name for the all-pervasive supreme Reality; also one of the Hindu trinity of gods, representing the Divine as the destroyer.

Shri: A term of respect, meaning "prosperity, wealth, glory, and success" and signifying mastery of all these.

Siddha: A perfected yogi; one who lives in unity consciousness.

smriti shāstra: (*lit.* remembered scriptures) The scriptural texts that are explanations, commentaries, and legends associated with the Vedas, which are the *shriti shāstra,* or "revealed scriptures" of India.

Swami: A respectful term of address for a *sannyāsin,* or monk.

Upanishads: The texts found at the end of each of the four Vedas, the most ancient of India's scriptures. Though different from one another in form, all Upanishads convey the same essential teaching: that the individual soul and God are one and that the realization of this Truth is the goal of human life.

Vaikuntha: The celestial abode of Lord Vishnu.

Further Reading

SWAMI MUKTANANDA

Play of Consciousness

From the Finite to the Infinite

Where Are You Going?

I Have Become Alive

The Perfect Relationship

Reflections of the Self

Secret of the Siddhas

I Am That

Kundalini

Mystery of the Mind

Does Death Really Exist?

Light on the Path

In the Company of a Siddha

Lalleshwari

Mukteshwari

Meditate

SWAMI CHIDVILASANANDA

My Lord Loves a Pure Heart

Kindle My Heart

Ashes at My Guru's Feet

You may learn more about the teachings and
practices of Siddha Yoga Meditation by contacting:

SYDA Foundation
371 Brickman Rd.
South Fallsburg, NY 12779-0600, USA

Tel: (914) 434-2000

or

Gurudev Siddha Peeth
P.O. Ganeshpuri
PIN 401 206
District Thana
Maharashtra, India

For further information about books in print
by Swami Muktananda and Swami Chidvilasananda,
and editions in translation, please contact:

Siddha Yoga Meditation Bookstore
371 Brickman Rd.
South Fallsburg, NY 12779-0600, USA

Tel: (914) 434-0124